LOVE & IDENTITY

~ 52 WEEKLY DEVOTIONALS ~

ADELE GROBLER

Ark House Press
PO Box 1722, Port Orchard, WA 98366 USA
PO Box 1321, Mona Vale NSW 1660 Australia
PO Box 318 334, West Harbour, Auckland 0661 New Zealand
arkhousepress.com

Cataloguing in Publication Data:
Title: Love and Identity
ISBN: 978-0-6454596-6-1 (pbk)
Subjects: Devotional;
Other Authors/Contributors: Grobler, Adele

Design by initiateagency.com

CONTENTS

ACKNOWLEDGMENT

This book is dedicated to my beautiful King Jesus, the One who showed me who I am and what I mean to Him. Without Your love, encouragement, strength and support, I would not be who I am today. So thank You my amazing King Jesus.

INTRODUCTION

As I have journeyed through life, I have found that having a revelation of your identity in Christ and His love for you are the vital components that establish you in an unshakable bond with Him. Most believers know that they are God's kids and that He says He loves them. For most, that is about the scope of their revelation. This is only the starting point of knowing who you are in Christ and His love for you. It was only when the Holy Spirit started to reveal my identity to me on a more personal level and Him providing greater revelation and encounters with His love in a way that I recognized that my entire world shifted. It was a process, and it was a journey. I would like to encourage you to never stop pursuing God in revealing more of who He says you are and who He sees you as. There are always more that He wants to show and reveal. I encourage you to keep asking Him to show you the deepest layers of His love for you in ways that you can recognize. Then, take whatever He shows you, receive it, believe it, and start making it a part of you by meditating on it and declaring it over your life. It is time for the body of Christ to know who they are in Him so that they can remain unshakable in a shakable world. These 52 devotionals are intended to help you grow in the understanding of your identity in Christ,

His love for you and your love for others over a one-year period. I would like to encourage you to not rush through the devotionals but rather to use them as intended. Read one devotional attentively each day during a one-week period. Take time to reflect, meditate and ponder on what is written. As you read it, ask the Holy Spirit to enlighten the eyes of your heart to greater understanding and revelation, and to help you to apply what you read and learn in your life. Doing it this way will allow for you to retain more of what you have read and learned, than if you rush through it. Know that you are truly loved and fearfully and wonderfully made!

NEW BEGINNINGS

I will put My Spirit in you, and you shall live, and I will
place you in your own land. Then you shall know that I,
the Lord, have spoken it and performed it, says the Lord.
Ezekiel 37:14 (NKJV)

Did last year take a toll on you, spiritually, emotionally, physically, and
mentally? Are you worn down and weary from the struggles you had to
face and endure? Did you find that you stopped "living" and switched over
to "survival mode" instead? You are not alone! Many went through hard
and challenging times. No matter how the year ended for you, a new year
is here. Allow God to refresh you, strengthen you, and heal you from the
struggles. It is time to live again! It is time to be refreshed in His Presence
so that you can thrive and run forward into all that He has for you in this
new year. Hold on to Him. Don't become complacent in your relationship
with Jesus this year. Seek Him more and be intentional about putting Him
first in everything. He will establish you and by the end of this new year,
when you look back, reflect on all that He did for you, as you will find that
His Spirit carried you and performed great wonders on your behalf. Part of
your identity in Christ is knowing that the Holy Spirit lives in you and He
helps you, leads and guides you. You are never alone in what you are facing.

You are not worthless, rejected, lonely or an outcast. You fit perfectly in unity with Him.

Declaration: God's Spirit gives me life.

2

THE HIGHEST-RANKING OFFICER

Therefore, God exalted Him to the highest place and
gave Him the name that is above every name.
Philippians 2:9 (NIV)

There are various ranks in the military. Each rank reports to a higher rank. Part of being a good soldier is knowing who your ranking officer is, the person you report to, and receive instructions from. Ranks are there to keep order. However, the general in the military has the highest authority and power. The general can override any instruction given by those who are inferior to the general's rank. This keeps other ranking officers in line. Likewise, the Lord put "ranks" in the earth for us to submit to. We submit to those ranks out of reverence and awe of God. For us, the highest rank is Jesus Christ Himself. He is the highest authority and power above any earthly rank that God put in position. As soldiers in God's army, we need to remember that even though we have "ranking officials" that are put in place for us to receive instructions from and to obey, we are still to follow God's orders above all. Human authority can be corrupted. God is incorruptible.

Declaration: There is no authority on earth that is supreme or higher than Jesus Christ.

3

A LEVEL OF EXCELLENCE

You have seen a person skilled in his work - he
will take his position before kings; he will not
take his position before obscure people.
Proverbs 22:29 (NET)

Sometimes we can get so caught up and focussed on our next goal, our next achievement, or our next pursuit, that we fail to sharpen the skill-sets and avenues that we already have. First bring your skills and current avenues up to a level of excellence. It might not always seem like there is much reward or much point in bringing our current skills and avenues up to a standard of excellence, especially when there is nothing in front of us to show us why we need to do it, for example, a promotion in the pipeline. What we sometimes fail to realize, is that it is not about doing it to receive a reward. What we are actually doing, is we are building foundations of excellence, so that the next skillset and avenue will stand firm and solid on that foundation. If you think about building a house, a house needs a firm and solid foundation otherwise the rest of the structure will not be sound. Don't just build for the present moment, think long term. Build with excellence.

Declaration: I focus to bring my current skillsets to a level of excellence.

4

HIS WAY IS YOUR BEST WAY

Again, this proves that God's choice doesn't depend
on how badly someone wants it or tries to earn it,
but it depends on God's kindness and mercy.
Romans 9:16 (TPT)

Have you ever tried to get something from God or make God do something by means of your own efforts? Have you prayed a bit extra and read an extra chapter in the Bible in the hopes that God will see the extra effort and move quicker in your life or answer a prayer quicker? I think most of us at one point in our life stepped into that trap, thinking our extra effort could somehow persuade God to want to move quicker. Chances are, if you have done this before, you felt frustrated, irritated and even discouraged as you put in effort only to not see the desired results. God does not think and respond like we do. God loves you and wants the best for you. God will choose to move and respond according to His will and purpose in our lives, and not necessarily according to our efforts or even our intense desire for it. Don't try and make things happen in your own strength. Rely on God, rest in Him, do what He says in His strength, be patient in the waiting. God always has your best interest in mind.

Declaration: I am patient in the waiting.

5

BE WILLING TO BE USED BY HIM

So pray to the Lord who is in charge of the harvest;
ask Him to send more workers into His fields.
Matthew 9:38 (NLT)

You might have heard this verse in *Matthew 9:38* being preached multiple times in church. The importance of us praying to God to send out "workers" to "work" in the "fields" of the "harvest" cannot be stressed enough. However, have you ever considered that you are the "worker" many generations before you have prayed for? To be used by God, to help bring people into His Kingdom, to be His messenger wherever you go so that the people around you can get to know Jesus? There are many roles that need to be filled during a harvest. You have supervising roles that ensure operations of harvesting run smoothly, there are those who are placed in position to cut the crops, those who go behind the cutters to gather the crops, those who organize the gathered crops and put them in storage for transportation, etc. During a harvest, all hands-on deck are required. Don't disqualify yourself because you think you don't fit a specific role. Be willing to be used by God. You have something God placed inside of you that others need.

Declaration: I am a willing worker in God's harvest field.

6

A TIME FOR PASSION AND A TIME FOR PAUSE

It is dangerous to have zeal without knowledge, and
the one who acts hastily makes poor choices.
Proverbs 19:2 (NET)

Have you ever been so on fire for God, driven by passion and enthusiasm that you just couldn't stop yourself from sharing, speaking, prophesying, doing, and acting upon the things God showed and revealed? Did you find that when you acted that spontaneously that what you shared, spoken, prophesied, and acted upon was not received well by others? Did you find yourself becoming discouraged in those moments and wanting to withdraw and then extinguish that fire in your heart because of the responses you received? If you have, then I want you to know that it is okay. The Bible teaches us that zeal (passion and enthusiasm) without knowledge is dangerous, as we tend to respond out of our emotions, which makes us act hastily and end up making poor choices of how we speak or when we speak. It is not wrong to have zeal for God and the things for God, but we also need knowledge to know when and how it is best to act. Don't allow the moments when you did it "incorrectly" to damage your identity in Christ. You are not your mistakes. Rather, your mistakes help you learn more about yourself. It shows you how you react when certain emotions are flared. This helps you to improve your responses so that your true identity in Christ shines through. So let go of the condemnation and guilt. You are forgiven.

Declaration: I don't make decisions in haste.

7

DON'T BECOME TOO RELAXED

Therefore, let the one who thinks he stands firm [immune
to temptation, being overconfident and self-righteous], take
care that he does not fall [into sin and condemnation].
1 Corinthians 10:12 (AMP)

Have you ever reached a point on your walk with Jesus where you thought
you might have conquered an issue, overcome a sin, or even reached a
certain height in your faith? You became "relaxed" or "comfortable" in that
space, perhaps thinking you won't fall back or backslide into the old issues
again or stumble in that faith? And then when you reached that point,
you let your guard down because you think you overcame and are strong
enough to resist? And then one day, all of a sudden, you find yourself deal-
ing with the same old issues again, or falling for the same temptation of
the same sin, or shrinking back in your faith? It happens to all of us. That
is why it is so important to not become complacent and relaxed when we
have "achieved" a certain level in the Lord. We should be confident in the
Lord to help us stand firm, but not overconfident in ourselves thinking we
won't stumble or fall, as Satan is always looking for ways to make us stumble. Part of your identity in Christ is knowing that you are nothing without

Him and you can do nothing without Him. Your confidence and identity is in Him and not your own abilities or strength.

Declaration: I take care not to become complacent in my walk with God.

8

FOCUS ON HIS OPINIONS, NOT THE WORLD'S

"This perfume could have been sold at a high price and the money given to the poor." Aware of this, Jesus said to them, "Why are you bothering this woman? She has done a beautiful thing to Me".
Matthew 26:9-10 (NIV)

Have you ever tried to do something for God out of the pureness of your heart, only to be ridiculed by others or rebuked by them because the way you were doing something for God did not fit their "box" of how things should be done? Did that make you feel "less than" and "unworthy" and like you didn't "measure up"? Making you wonder if what you were doing was truly acceptable to God based on other people's opinions of the situation? Well, if you have then you are in good company. That is how the disciples treated the woman with the alabaster jar. They looked with worldly eyes instead of spiritual eyes. They were more concerned with the logical uses of the perfume rather than seeing the blessing that it was to Jesus. Jesus came to her defence and stood up for her. He made sure His disciples knew that what she did was something wonderful to Him. So don't retreat. Bless the Lord with all the pureness of your heart. You were created uniquely and so your expression of affection towards Him will be unique to you as well.

Declaration: I bless my God from the pureness of my heart.

9

GIVE HIM YOUR BURDENS

For My yoke is easy and My burden is light.
Matthew 11:30 (NIV)

Have you ever wondered what this verse means? How can a yoke and a burden be light? If you think about oxen, when they are yoked together to pull a carriage or equipment, the yoke that is put on them is very heavy. And the burdens of the world are heavy to carry. So how is it that God's yoke is easy and His burden light? It is because you don't carry it alone. Jesus does the heavy lifting. The Kingdom assignments, instructions, commands and requirements He gives us all come with the help of the Holy Spirit to lead, guide and help us to carry it. He never puts a "yoke" or "burden" on us and expects us to carry it alone without any help. Whereas the "yokes" and "burdens" of the world are heavy as they are not "yoked" together with Jesus, and so those who align with the "yokes" and "burdens" of the world, need to carry them alone.

Declaration: God helps me carry my burdens.

10

WHERE HE IS, DARKNESS FLEES

For you are all children of the light and children of the
day. We don't belong to the night nor to darkness.
1 Thessalonians 5:5 (TPT)

When you have given your life to Christ, you have crossed over from death to life. You are no longer a part of the darkness that is in the world. People who have not yet made the decision to surrender their life to Christ and follow Him, are still living in the darkness. We are children of the Light. That does not mean that we live in a light environment. In fact, we are living surrounded by darkness, but God's light is in us. Don't let anyone deceive you when they say you belong to the darkness because your surroundings look dark. Know in your heart the truth, that you have no control over whether light or dark surrounds you. You only have control over the light that is in you. Only you have control over the decisions you make including your decision to follow Christ. Making a mistake or accidentally sinning does not automatically make you a child of darkness when you have given your life to Christ. He died to drain out the darkness.

Declaration: God's light shines in me.

PLACE YOUR HOPES IN HIM

Rejoice in hope, be patient in tribulation, be constant in prayer.
Romans 12:12 (ESV)

Have you ever read this verse and thought how it is possible to always rejoice in hope? The Bible says in Proverbs 13:12 that hope deferred makes the heart sick. So how can we always rejoice in hope when our hopes aren't always met and hope deferred sets in? The answer is found in Psalm 42:11 where David writes to not be down cast but to put your hope in God. It is not wrong to hope for things or to hope that circumstances and situations will change, but if we hope in those things more than we hope in God, our hopes may become deferred as we place our hopes on earthly things that will perish and fade. But when we place our hope in God, our expectation of encountering Him and our feeling of trust in Him, our hopes won't be put to shame as it says in Romans 5:5. God is stable and never changing. So, if you have experienced hope deferred, examine your heart and see what your hopes are based on and re-adjust your focus. Remember, this life is only temporary, but you get to spend eternity with God. How amazing is that!

Declaration: I put my hope in God before anything else.

12

MIND YOUR FAMILY

But if anyone does not provide for his relatives, and
especially for members of his household, he has
denied the faith and is worse than an unbeliever.
1 Timothy 5:8 (ESV)

Family is important. You might not like the one you have, but it is the one God gave you. God expects us to take care of our relatives, to provide for them. Providing and caring for our relatives can look many ways. It could be through financial blessing, helping them clean their home, helping them to fix their car, showing them love and support, taking them for their doctor's appointment etc. We can sometimes get so busy helping other people who are in need around us that we can sometimes miss the need in our own homes and families. We should not neglect taking care of those God has given us for the sake of others. This is not balanced and not how God created the family to function. If needs are met amongst relatives, it removes the need for their needs to be met by someone else. If your family needs money and they don't steward well, perhaps you can buy the items they need instead.

Declaration: I take care of my family and I make them a priority.

13

"RE-SEASON" YOUR FLAVOUR

You are the salt of the earth; but if the salt loses its flavour,
how shall it be seasoned? It is then good for nothing but
to be thrown out and trampled underfoot by men.
Matthew 5:13 (NKJV)

Has life knocked out the saltiness and flavour you bring to those around you? Where you once were so excited about God and the exciting things He was doing, spreading joy, hope and peace all around? And now you find yourself drained, discouraged, hopeless and even numb and lifeless at times? Life can knock us down pretty hard. It can feel like there is no hope or no end to our sufferings. We kind of have to wonder how the disciples were able to be joyful under intense persecution and trials. I believe it is because they tapped into a little "secret". It is to go up "higher". Going up higher with Jesus during those times. It means that no matter what the external circumstances are like, you understand that even though you are on the earth, you are not of the earth. You live seated in heavenly places with Jesus. You tap into His joy, the joy of spending time in His presence, which releases unexplainable joy in your life and "re-seasons" your flavour.

Declaration: Even when life is hard, I will still keep my flavour and saltiness.

14

HE WILL NEVER FORSAKE YOU

I will remember the deeds of the Lord; yes, I
will remember Your miracles of long ago.
Psalm 77:11 (NIV)

God does not only perform miracles on our behalf to give us the break-throughs we need, but He brings those miraculous breakthroughs to teach us something about His nature and His love toward us. We were not created to live from miracle to miracle. If we do, we leave ourselves open to discouragement and despair, believing God does not love us if He does not bring the breakthrough miracle we need. We see this happen to the Israelites over and over again. They received the breakthrough miracles, however, they failed to receive the revelation of God as their Provider and Protector and failed to see His love in the miracles. So, every time they found themselves in hairy situations, they were quick to forget God's heart towards them and ended up pleading for miracles again. It is not wrong to ask for miracles and breakthroughs, but just remember what God has previously done for you, knowing He is with you in all things. How much God loves and values you are not related to you receiving breakthroughs. Moses did not receive the breakthrough in being able to enter the promised land, and yet God called him His friend. Learn to separate "who you are" and how much God loves you from the circumstances you find yourself in.

Declaration: When I am struggling, I remember how God came through previously, so I take heart and wait on Him.

I5

TRUST HIS PLANS FOR YOU

So he said to Him, "O my Lord, how can I save Israel? Indeed my clan
is the weakest in Manasseh, and I am the least in my father's house."
Judges 6:15 (NKJV)

When God calls you or asks you do to something for Him, do you bring
up your list of all the reasons why He should not be asking or calling
you? Listing off the things of why you are not qualified enough. Things
such as "I don't speak very well", "I don't dress as they do", "I am not smart
enough", "I don't have enough resources", I don't know how to do it", I am
a sinful person", "I am weak", "there are others that qualify way better for
the job" etc. If you are someone who keeps disqualifying yourself or make
excuses as to why you cannot do what God asks you to do, then I would
like to encourage you to stop that today. It is human nature to feel over-
whelmed when God gives you a great task. But just remember that God is
also the One who created you and knows what He put inside you. Gideon
and Moses felt the same. They both gave God their reasons for why they
should not be called, and yet God accomplished great feats through them.
God puts "gold" in us that we don't always see. God knows who we are and
what we are capable of. Trust His view of your character, and not your own.

Declaration: I do not disqualify myself when God calls me to do His works.

16

DO NOT BECOME COMPLACENT

If My people, which are called by My name, shall humble
themselves, and pray, and seek My face, and turn from
their wicked ways; then will I hear from heaven, and
will forgive their sin, and will heal their land.

2 Chronicles 7:14 (KJV)

Complacency is a massive problem in the body of Christ. Many have become "dull" or "numb" in their prayer life. Many do not rise up and pray and intercede for others, their cities, or their nations. Imagine what would happen if every believer in the world would stand up and stand unified together in prayer for their cities, nations, and families. As a son and daughter of God, we are tasked to have dominion over the earth. Our battle is not against flesh and blood but against the dark forces at work. God is looking for His people to stand in the gap. To not fall asleep when prayer is most needed. God understands when we are tired. Jesus did not hold it against His disciples when they fell asleep in the garden when He asked them to keep watch and pray, for He understood their weakness. But let us not make it a habit to not show up and stand in the gap. Our prayers are powerful and are needed. God shows up for us. Let us show up for God.

Declaration: I take care not to become complacent in the Kingdom of God.

17

FORGIVE AS YOU WISH TO BE FORGIVEN

Then came Peter to Him and said, Lord, how often
shall my brother sin against me, and I forgive him? Till
seven times? Jesus saith unto him, I say not unto thee,
until seven times: but, until seventy times seven.
Matthew 18:21-22 (KJV)

Let me ask you something, how often do you sin? How often do you disobey God? How often do you make mistakes, saying the wrong thing, making wrong choices? It is very confronting to think about it. We would rather not. Now, let me ask you, how often does God forgive you through Christ for your sins? Does He forgive you every time you are sorry for your offenses and ask forgiveness and turn from your sin? Does He forgive you? Of course, He does! That is why Jesus came, to die for our sins, to remove our guilt. 1 John 1:9 says that if we confess our sins, He is faithful and just to forgive us and to cleanse us from all unrighteousness. Now let me ask you a harder question, how often do you forgive those who sin against you? Forgiveness does not mean you give approval to wrong that has been done. Forgiveness means you don't harbor resentment and hatred in your heart, but to show mercy to those who sinned against you. God says to forgive as He forgives us. Just remember, you are not the sum of the offences that were committed against you. Rip that label off! You are a precious son and daughter of the Most High God.

Declaration: I forgive because God forgives me.

18

DISCIPLINE OUT OF LOVE

If anyone stirs up strife, it is not from Me; whoever
stirs up strife with you shall fall because of you.
Isaiah 54:15 (ESV)

God does discipline and rebuke us in love when we are out of alignment or agreement with Him. God can use different things to do this, it does not always look the same. He can discipline us through circumstances, He can rebuke us through His Word, regardless of the many ways in which He can bring discipline and correction, He will not use strife through a person to do this. Isaiah 54:15 says that if anyone should stir up strife with you, it is not God's doing. Proverbs 6:16-19 talks about the six things the Lord hates, and seven that are detestable to Him. One of them in verse 19 is a person who stirs up conflict and strife amongst people. So, if you have found yourself in contention with someone, and people are telling you the Lord sends them to rebuke you or discipline you, know that this is not in alignment with God's Word. God can certainly teach you through it, but it is not sent by Him as a form of discipline.

Declaration: Strife is not from God, so I make every effort to keep peace.

19

GOD WILL AVENGE YOU

*If your enemy is hungry, give him food to eat; if he is
thirsty, give him water to drink. In doing this, you will heap
burning coals on his head, and the Lord will reward you.*
Proverbs 25:21-22 (NIV)

The bible teaches us that God is our Avenger, and we should make room
for His revenge upon our enemies, rather than taking it upon ourselves.
It is a hard thing to process and do, especially when we have been deeply
wronged. We do feel to justify ourselves and fight back. Well, there is a way
that you can do that. A way that is pleasing to God and a way that will also
"get back" at your enemies, and that is to do good to them. Remember,
behind every person that wronged you is a bigger enemy, Satan, who comes
to kill, steal and destroy in your life. Satan hates everything good, he expects
you to retaliate with anger, offense, unforgiveness, unkindness, disrespect
etc. In fact, he counts on it, because he wants you to sin so that you will
bring even further destruction in your life. Don't give him that satisfaction,
move in the opposite spirit and do good and right to your enemies, for that
pleases God and God promises to reward you for it.

Declaration: I do good to my enemies and not evil.

20

BE AN AMBASSADOR FOR CHRIST

Jesus said to His disciples: "Things that cause
people to sin are bound to come, but woe to
that person through whom they come.
Luke 17:1 (NIV)

In 2 Corinthians 5:20, it says that we are Christ's ambassadors. It is a great honour to represent our beautiful King Jesus to those around us. It is an honour and a privilege that should not be taken for granted. The world is to see Christ in us. Part of your identity is being an ambassador of Christ. Therefore, we are to live lives worthy of that call. Every word we speak, every action we do, every thought we think, should be done with Christ in mind. Do you represent Christ well to those around you? Or are you someone who claims to be His follower and disciple, and yet you deliberately sin and teach others to do the same? Disregarding the Word of God for the sake or your own fleshly desires and will? As Luke 17:1 says, woe to that person through whom sins come to others. Repent today if that is you. Don't teach others to give way to sinful ways. Rather teach them in accordance with God's Word, which brings life. Make sure you practise what you preach.

Declaration: As an ambassador for Christ, I make an effort to lead by example.

21

HIDE IN HIM

The name of the Lord is a strong tower; the
righteous run to it and are safe.
Proverbs 18:10 (KJV)

God is and loves to be our safe hiding place. When we come into God's presence it is like we enter into a shielded and private space, where all the noise of the world and the day quiets down. It is in that place where we, as sons and daughters of God, can be real, open, honest and safe. It is in that place where you can have conversations with Jesus about anything and everything that is on your heart. He listens and loves it when you open up your heart to Him, not hiding anything from Him. Even though He knows it all already He still wants to hear about it. Spending time in God's presence also "shields" us from the spiritual forces of evil for they cannot stand to be in God's presence. Make the Lord your refuge in times of trouble. Go to a quiet place and pray to Him. He can handle everything you share with Him. He is very strong and powerful, He understands your heart.

Declaration: God is my fortress and my safe place.

22

WHAT SATAN DESTROYS, GOD RESTORES

The thief comes only to steal and kill and destroy; I have
come that they may have life, and have it to the full.
John 10:10 (NIV)

The devil prowls around like a roaring lion looking for someone to devour (1 Peter 5:8). Even though Satan is out to kill, steal and destroy in our lives, we can be confident and assured that no matter what he targets us with, God can turn all of it around for our good. Proverbs 6:30-31 says that if a thief is caught, he must pay seven-fold back, even if it costs him all he has. I have learned by now to claim back seven-fold from what Satan tries to steal from me. I no longer sit and just take the punches, instead I make it very expensive for the enemy to steal from me. God always has our back. When we bring our case before Him, He hears us and defends our cause. He no longer sees the sins and wrongdoing Satan accuses us with when we have asked God to forgive us, for Jesus covered us in His blood, that is why we can come with confidence to the His throne of grace and receive mercy and grace for help in our times of need. Part of your identity is knowing that you are made righteous through Jesus' sacrifice and therefore you are acceptable to God.

Declaration: When Satan steals from me, I claim sevenfold back in Jesus Name.

23

ALLOW GOD TO CONVICT YOU
IN YOUR DAILY ACTIONS

And whatever you do, in word or deed, do everything in the name
of the Lord Jesus, giving thanks to God the Father through Him.
Colossians 3:17 (ESV)

Are you mindful of the Holy Spirit as you go about your day? Do you think about the Lord during the day, and are you conscious of Him when you make decisions about what you are spending your time doing, the conversations you partake in and how you do your work? God sees and knows everything we do and speak. What will He find when He listens to the way you speak? Will He hear you gossiping, slandering, judging others and partake in other ungodly conversations? Or will He hear you speak life giving, godly and encouraging words and conversations? What will God see you watching on television? Will it be content full of violence and sensuality, or will it be decent content drawing you closer to Him? What will God see you do at your workplace? Will He see you cut corners, being dishonest, and treating your boss or colleagues with contempt? Or will He find you doing the right thing at your workplace? Some food for thought.

Declaration: I work and speak as though I am doing it for Jesus.

24

LIFE IS IN HIM, NOT IN THIS WORLD

And I say to you, My friends, do not be afraid of those who kill
the body and after that have no more that they can do. But I
will show you whom you should fear: Fear Him who, after has
killed, has power to cast into hell: yes, I say to you, fear Him!
Luke 12:4-5 (NKJV)

A s followers of Jesus, we need not act like the rest of the world in relation to what is happening around us. Those in the world without Jesus, live in fear, despair, hopelessness, discouragement and fear of what man can do to them. The Bible teaches us to take heart for Jesus has overcome the world and to rejoice in the Lord. The reason for this is that Jesus already died and suffered for us so that those who believe in Him will have eternal life. Unlike the world who does not have Jesus, we know that if we should depart from this life, we have a better and eternal life waiting for us. It is like it says in Philippians 1:21 - to live is Christ and to die is gain. So, we make the most out of every day and opportunity by investing in our relationship with God and doing those good works He prepared in advance for us to do and when our time comes, we get to be with Him forever. Now that is a lasting hope.

Declaration: I do not fear what man can do to me; eternal life is found in Jesus.

25

A FRIEND OF THE KING

You are My friends if you do what I command. I no longer
call you servants, because a servant does not know his master's
business. Instead, I have called you friends, for everything
that I learned from My Father I have made known to you.
John 15:14-15 (NIV)

True friendship is priceless. If you have ever had a true friend, you would understand the rarity and the beauty of it. We all have had friendships. Some close, some not so close. The closeness of our friendships is determined by both parties. Healthy friendships require balance. If one party keeps on "taking" more and the other party "giving" more, there is an imbalance, and the one who "gives" more might end up feeling resentful because the other party does not invest as much in the relationship. Friendships can be fickle. Friendships come and go. Others stay and last for years. There is one Friend who will always remain constant, loyal, loving and eternal, and that is Jesus. How amazing is it that we are called friends of God when we obey His commands? If this day you feel like you have no friends, take heart, for you always have a friend in Jesus.

Declaration: I am a friend of God.

26

A FATHER DISCIPLINES HIS CHILDREN

And have you forgotten the divine word of encouragement
which is addressed to you as sons, "My son, do not make
light of the discipline of the Lord, and do not lose heart
and give up when you are corrected by Him.
Hebrews 12:5 (AMP)

Any good earthly father disciplines and corrects his children out of love. If a child acts inappropriately, disrespectfully, and continually does the wrong thing, the father will chastise the child because he knows that the behaviour his child is portraying will lead down a path of destruction. There are times the father will speak gently to their child, but if the child refuses to listen, the father becomes firmer and sterner in the way he will correct, address and discipline the child so that they will heed and turn from the error of their way. Likewise with God. God is gracious, kind, loving, generous, merciful, and long-suffering. He loves us incredibly. But if we, like a child, continue to ignore His corrections, He will at times become stern and firm in how He speaks, corrects, and disciplines us. We are not to despise it when the Lord corrects us, because He is treating us as sons and daughters. Receive His love and correction.

Declaration: When God disciplines me, it is because He loves me and wants the best for me.

27

ENCOURAGE OTHERS, AND BE ENCOURAGED

Your words have upheld him who was stumbling,
and you have strengthened the feeble knees.
Job 4:4 (NKJV)

2 Corinthians 1:4 says that God comforts us in our troubles so that we may be able to comfort others in their troubles. God gives us what we need to help others and He also shows us what that looks like. We can make it our aim to be intentional in helping and supporting others. However, there are times when we are unaware of the impact we have. You might not necessarily give thought to giving a compliment to someone, you just do it without thinking. Little do you know that compliment might have meant the world to them and changed the course of their life or their outlook. When we pray and ask for God to use us for His purposes, He does. He will fill your mouth with the right words for the right time for the person who needs it. You won't always get feedback from them, but God sees the impact. Always be ready to comfort, support, and encourage another.

Declaration: I encourage others.

28

HE WILL HELP CARRY YOUR BURDENS

Bear one another's burdens, and so fulfill the law of Christ.
For if anyone thinks he is something, when he is nothing,
he deceives himself. But let each one test his own work, and
then his reason to boast will be in himself alone and not in
his neighbour. For each will have to bear his own load.
Galatians 6:2-5 (ESV)

The Bible teaches us that we are to carry each other's burdens but also that we will need to carry our own load. Every person you meet will be carrying a burden of their own. We are to help each other, support, and love one another, however, you were not created to carry the burdens of the world on your shoulders. That is Jesus' job. When you carry a burden, the first thing you need to do is take it to Jesus and cast your care on Him. In exchange, receive His help and His peace over your burden and ask Him how to manage it. Then you can share your burden with others. The Bible says to commit our way to the Lord and then our plans will succeed. People are imperfect and they don't always give the right advice nor have the capacity to keep carrying your burden. God is the one with the answers to your situation. If you ask Him about your burdens, He will show you what to do with them. You will also then be able to evaluate if another person's advice agrees with what God has already spoken to you.

Declaration: I give my burdens to Jesus.

29

LET THE HOLY SPIRIT SPEAK THROUGH YOU

Brethren, if anyone among you wanders from the truth, and someone turns him back, let him know that he who turns a sinner from the error of his way will save a soul from death and cover a multitude of sins.
James 5:19-20 (NKJV)

When you see your brother or sister in Christ sinning, being deceived, or not walking in truth, don't be too quick to judge them and accuse them of wrongdoing. Firstly, remember that you also sin and fall short in many ways. You are not perfect either. The Bible says that judgment without mercy will be shown to anyone who has not been merciful, mercy triumphs over judgment. We are to help and bring correction in love. That is why it is so important to ask the Holy Spirit for wisdom in how you are to address your brother or sister and the issue at hand. Love and gentleness bring restoration. Harsh words and accusations bring conflict and separation. Ask them why they are doing what they are doing, don't just assume. Sometimes there is a reason for it, and it can be rooted in deep hurts from their past. Take an interest first. Gently find out the reason, and let the Holy Spirit fill your mouth with the right things to say.

Declaration: I gently correct, under the leading of the Holy Spirit, my brother or sister in Christ when they fall into sin.

30

LET HIM CORRECT THE INJUSTICES

Do not take revenge, my dear friends, but leave
room for God's wrath, for it is written: "It is
Mine to avenge; I will repay, says the Lord.
Romans 12:19 (NIV)

We have all experienced injustice to some degree. When we have been wronged, we tend to want to retaliate. There is a time and a season for everything, as it says in Ecclesiastes chapter 3. We have to use discernment in these times we are living in. Sometimes we have to speak up, sometimes we have to remain silent. At no point does God ask of us to harm or hurt our enemies when they have harmed and hurt us. Jesus teaches us to turn the other cheek, to forgive, to remain kind, loving and compassionate. To show mercy and to be gentle. This does not mean that we are a door mat for people to walk all over. But this does mean that we need to keep our hearts and minds pure and in alignment with God's will no matter what. God says that it is for Him to avenge us for the wrong that has been done to us. He is the best avenger, and He does a better job than you even could. Surrender the injustice to God, ask Him to avenge you. Ask Him what you are to do about the situation, to leave it, or to address it.

Declaration: I leave room for God to fight against my enemies.

31

FIRST LOVE

Yet I hold this against you: you have forsaken your
first love. Remember the height from which you have
fallen! Repent and do the things you did at first.
Revelations 2:4-5 (NIV)

When you read Revelation Chapter 2 you see that God was commending the church in Ephesus for their deeds, their hard work, and their perseverance. However, they forgot about their relationship with God and were more focused on doing the "works" than cultivating that relationship with Him. That is why He said to them in verses 4-5, to repent and turn back to Him. Similarly, when you read Matthew 7:21-23, Jesus made it clear that it is not by "works" that we will be saved. He wants us to know Him and Him to know us. Sometimes we can become so distracted by doing good deeds for God, that we don't have time to spend in His presence. That is not God's will. God has always been for relationship first. When you make time to build your relationship with God, you will then know and understand better the work and deeds He has for you to do. You then operate from a place of grace and rest, able to do it all. Part of your identity in Christ is knowing that you are the bride of Christ. A bride makes time for her husband and makes him a priority.

Declaration: I put my relationship with God first.

32

ALLOW HIM TO TRANSFORM YOU

And we who with unveiled faces all reflect the Lord's glory
are being transformed into His likeness with ever-increasing
glory, which comes from the Lord, who is the Spirit.
2 Corinthians 3:18 (NIV)

When we have given our lives to God and received Jesus as our living Lord and Saviour, God starts and continues to work on our character to become more like Him. He starts to "purify" and "burn" away those parts in our natural state that do not align with Him and His ways, and He helps mould us into something better. The transformation process is not always a pleasant one as it requires us to deny our flesh and our own wants and interests that do not align with God's best for our lives, but the process is so worth it. Allow God to do the work He wants to do in your life. If you are not sure where to start or how to become more like Him, just go to the Bible. The Bible is the Living Word, containing everything we need for life and godliness through Christ Jesus our Lord. We are God's ambassadors on the earth. We testify to His goodness and His work in our lives.

Declaration: I am being transformed into God's likeness.

33

"AGE" IS NOT YOUR IDENTITY

But the Lord said to me, "Do not say, 'I am too young.' You must
go to everyone I send you to and say whatever I command you.
Jeremiah 1:7 (NIV)

Have you discredited yourself from being used by God because of your age? Have you had people come up against you saying you are too young to step out and do what God is asking you to do, and then those lies have kept you held and bound from moving forward? Or perhaps people have told you that you are too old to accomplish things for the Lord, and the work should rather be left to those younger as they bring more fresh and current ideas? Whether you feel you are too young or too old to be used by God, it makes no difference. When God calls you, He calls you. He is well aware of your age, your knowledge, your life experience etc. God does not look at the things man looks at. He uses young children to lay hands on the sick and heal them. He uses the elderly to take "territory" for the Kingdom. Don't allow people's viewpoints or perspectives to stop you. Obey God and follow Him. You are not what your "age" dictates. Your "age" is not your identity. God is looking for willing hearts.

Declaration: I am never too young or too old to be used by God; He knows my age.

34

YOU ARE HIS BELOVED CHILD

I will not leave you as orphans; I will come to you.
John 14:18 (NIV)

We don't have to be orphans according to the standard of this world to carry an orphan spirit. You still might have both your parents and grown up in a loving home, and still feel like an orphan in your spirit when it comes to God. You might have fear and doubt that God won't take care of your needs, or that perhaps He will abandon you if you don't do your Christian walk perfectly. You might fear that He is mad at you and will scold you if you misstep. That is not God's heart for you. God adopts us as sons and daughters when we believe in Jesus Christ who died and rose again for us. God's heart is for family and community. He will never push you away when you come to Him, no matter what you have done. Philippians 4:19 says that God will supply all our needs, not our wants, but our needs. He won't leave you helpless, but He will show you the way forward. Trust Him! You are not an orphan.

Declaration: I am grafted into God's family and God is my Father who meets all my needs; He is always there for me.

35

RISE ABOVE ARGUMENTS

Don't have anything to do with foolish and stupid arguments, because
you know they produce quarrels. And the Lord's servant must not quarrel;
instead, he must be kind to everyone, able to teach, not resentful.

2 Timothy 2:23 (NIV)

Have you ever had those conversations whether it be with family, friends, or colleagues, that seem to stir up anger, frustration, and strife in your heart? These conversations could be due to differences in viewpoints and opinions about politics, priorities in a work project, decisions regarding social inter-actions, and so forth. Have you noticed your voice becoming a bit harsher in tone, and your body language starting to show your disapproval during those conversations? Have you noticed how quickly fights break out between the parties if the matter is not dropped or re-directed? The Bible teaches us to have nothing to do with foolish and stupid arguments because if we don't drop those matters or resolve them quickly, they end up in a fight. We say things we don't mean, or we say things in a manner that hurts others. It is for our benefit to not provoke such situations, to rather walk away and agree to disagree. Know who you are in Christ. This will help you be secure in who you are so that you don't always feel the need to have to defend yourself.

Declaration: I make it my aim to not provoke fights with others.

36

HAVE FAITH IN HIS FAITHFULNESS

If we are faithless, He remains faithful [true to His word and
His righteous character], for He cannot deny Himself.
2 Timothy 2:13 (AMP)

We all have had experiences in life where people we trusted or relied upon broke faith with us. These experiences are not pleasant, and it leaves a "mark" on our hearts. When we don't receive healing from the Lord, these "marks" never heal, and it can obscure our understanding of God's nature and faithfulness to us. We then respond out of our experiences in life, rather than on truth. People are imperfect. No one person will be able to be faithful 100% of the time. God is perfect. He is the same yesterday, today, and forever! He never changes. So, when God promises us in His Word that He will remain faithful to us, even when we don't remain faithful to Him, we can be assured that what He says is true. Don't be like the people who broke faith with you and so break faith with God. Be faithful, loyal, and committed to Him for He loves you incredibly and is always there for you.

Declaration: God always remains faithful to me, no matter what. His faithfulness is based on His constant, unchanging nature.

37

FOCUS DAILY ON THE GOOD RATHER THAN THE BAD

Do everything without complaining or arguing, so that you may become
blameless and pure, children of God without fault in a crooked and
depraved generation, in which you shine like stars in the universe.
Philippians 2:14-15 (NIV)

Society culture tells us that it is okay to complain when things don't go
our way or when we are inconvenienced. There is an emphasis on "self"
and "entitlement". Did you know that complaining is offensive to God? In
the Old Testament we can see how the Lord rebuked the Israelites for their
complaining and unbelief. Complaining is a sign of discontentment. In 1
Timothy 6:6-11 it says that godliness with contentment is great gain and
that we should be content with what we have, for we brought nothing into
this world, and we can take nothing out of it. As children of God, we are
created in His image and are to follow Jesus' example on the earth. We are
lights in a dark world and are called to live lives according to God and not
according to the world. We need to lead by example. Instead of focussing on
what you don't have, think about what you do have and thank God for it.

Declaration: When I am tempted to complain, I reflect on all the good
things God has done and praise Him for it instead.

38

YOU ARE UNIQUE, AND GOD UTILISES THAT

But God chose the foolish things of the world to shame the wise; God
chose the weak things of the world to shame the strong. He chose the
lowly things of this world and the despised things - and the things that are
not - to nullify the things that are, so that no one may boast before Him.
1 Corinthians 1:27-29 (NIV)

God can use anyone. He is not limited to qualifications, experience,
expertise, positions, or titles. So, if you have been thinking that you
have nothing to offer God, think again! God's power is revealed in our
weaknesses. He equips us with everything we need. It is not about "feeling"
equipped, "ready" or even "prepared". It is about what is true and what
God calls you to do. You are never alone on this life's journey. So don't discredit yourself, even if others might. God makes a way where there seems to
be none! It is also important that you don't discredit others. Be very careful
not to look down on anyone that God calls and uses. God does not take it
kindly when we raise our hands or voices against His anointed ones. So be
mindful to not judge another just because they don't "fit" the picture that
you might have in your mind. Be merciful, just like God has been merciful
towards you. Embrace your uniqueness and the uniqueness of others.

Declaration: God can use me.

39

USE THE HOLY SPIRIT AS YOUR GUIDE

But now, by dying to what once bound us, we have been
released from the law so that we serve in the new way of
the Spirit, and not in the old way of the written code.
Romans 7:6 (NIV)

Jesus came to fulfill the law so that we can live in the new way of grace. It is not through the law that we are saved but through Jesus. The law and commandments help us to understand what sin is and what God's heart is for us regarding the ways we are to live. Living by the Holy Spirits' promptings, directions and instructions help us to overcome the continued sins we commit. Just like Jesus saved us from the law that bound us, so is He able to save and free us from habitual sins. All you have to do is ask the Holy Spirit to help you, keep you accountable, and then follow in obedience. Whatever He asks you to change and let go of, do so, otherwise you will remain stuck in your old ways. Our flesh needs to die, which can be painful, but as you keep dying to your old sinful ways, your spirit man becomes stronger and then you will find you tend to live more righteously. You are not your sin.

Declaration: I live by the Spirit and so can overcome my habitual sins.

40

EVERY PERSON IS WONDER-FULLY AND FEARFULLY MADE

After this I looked and there before me was a great multitude
that no-one could count, from every nation, tribe, people and
language, standing before the throne and in front of the Lamb.
Revelation 7:9 (NIV)

You might have heard it being said that God is not a respecter of persons - Acts 10:34. God created each one with their skin colour and He knew exactly what nation each one will belong to. God even gave each their language - Genesis chapter 11. In Revelations 7:9 it is clear that there will be more than one nation, race and language that will stand before our beautiful Jesus. So, if you have been told that Jesus does not love you and that you won't fit in in heaven because of your nationality, skin colour or background, please know that it is not true. God created you the way you are specifically for Him. Jesus died for the sins of the world and not just for one nation, race or people. We are family and should treat each other that way. Love the way Jesus loves. Let us make an effort to make each other feel welcomed, seen and known. Do not raise your heel against your brother or sister when the Lord has approved them. Your identity remains in Christ regardless of your skin colour, nationality, or culture.

Declaration: No matter what nation, language or race I come from, God created me and counts me worthy of His love.

41

WE ARE INTERCONNECTED

In Him the whole building is joined together and rises to become
a holy temple in the Lord. And in Him you too are being built
together to become a dwelling in which God lives by His Spirit.
Ephesians 2:21-22 (NIV)

You are the dwelling place where the Holy Spirit chooses to abide in.
How incredible is that! Of all the places God could have chosen, He
chose to dwell inside us. All believers, those who accepted Jesus as Lord and
Saviour of their lives, are continually being built together to become a holy
temple in the Lord. This means that it is a process. Building takes time and
as with every building project, sometimes there are a few things that need
to be re-adjusted, broken down and re-built, and finishing touches need to
be applied. None of us are exempt of the process of building. As we submit
ourselves to our faithful Creator, continuing to do what is good and follow-
ing Him, we start to see how the Body is interconnected. We all need each
other. We all have different gifts, talents and skills which work together in
unison to bring glory to God the Father. Know that as part of your identity,
is that you are the residing place (temple) for the Holy Spirit.

Declaration: I am a temple in which the Holy Spirit dwells in.

42

YOU HAVE AUTHORITY THROUGH CHRIST

I have given you authority to trample on snakes and scorpions and
to overcome all the power of the enemy; nothing will harm you.
Luke 10:19 (NIV)

Do you know that you have authority over the enemy in your life? Do
you know that you do not have to listen and believe every lie the enemy
tells you or shows you? Sometimes Christians feel so defeated because of
the spiritual warfare they experience, but they forget that Jesus triumphed
over the enemy and has given them His victory to walk in. The Bible tells
us that we can trample on snakes and scorpions and overcome all the power
of the enemy. The Lord would not have made that statement if it was not
a necessity for us to believe and walk-in. When we partner with the Holy
Spirit and ask Him about the warfare we are facing and the strategies to
overcome, He will reveal and help us. When we align with His truth and
guidance our spiritual wellbeing is not harmed, for we do not compromise
the truth God has given and spoken to us in exchange to believe lies from
the enemy. Know that as a child of God, you have the authority in Christ
to overcome the enemy's schemes. You are powerful and not powerless in
Christ. So stand your ground against the attacks of the enemy.

Declaration: I am not a defeated child of God; I have authority in Christ.

43

GOD KNOWS WHO YOU ARE

When the angel of the Lord appeared to Gideon, he
said, "the Lord is with you, mighty warrior."
Judges 6:12 (NIV)

God knows who you are even if you don't yet. The world around us try and tell us who we are, or whom they want and expect us to be. When you examine the life of Gideon in the Bible, you will find that he did not think much of himself. He saw himself as the least in his family and also that his tribe was the least in comparison to others. When the angel of the Lord appeared to Gideon, telling him that he was a mighty warrior and that God was sending him to save Israel, it greatly perplexed him as that was not whom he believed he was or what others saw when they looked at him. Your identity lies in whom Daddy-God says you are, and not what you might think or feel about yourself. God sees the treasure, talents, gifts and heart that He has placed within you. Ask Him to show and reveal to you, who you are. Receive what He shows you in humility. Don't discredit it in false humility. It is never a wise thing to tell God that He is wrong about you since He created you and knows you best. So throw off false humility and accept with a grateful and thankful heart that God appreciates the awesome you that you are.

Declaration: My God knows who I am; I receive my identity from Him and not from the world around me.

44

YOU ARE HIS CHILD

As a mother comforts her child, so will I comfort
you; and you will be comforted over Jerusalem.
Isaiah 66:13 (NIV)

We sometimes forget the tenderness of God's heart towards us. We can get caught up in our human mentality of what we think an earthly father looks like. Some earthly fathers are really gentle and good nurturers, but mostly when we think of fathers, we think of someone who is strong, a protector, and not necessarily tender and nurturing. That is more a picture we get when we think of mothers. God is all we need and more. He is not limited in how He can meet our needs. He is our ultimate comforter and nurturer. So, if today you feel the need for comfort and you seem to have none in your world you can receive comfort from, run to Daddy-God. Receive His mercy, love, tenderness and compassion towards you. He should be the first go to for every need you have. He knows your heart, your pain, your struggles and your battles.

Declaration: God is my ultimate comforter; I run to Him when I need support.

45

YOU HAVE NO COMPETITION

Looking unto Jesus, the Author and Finisher of our faith, who for
the joy that was set before Him endured the cross, despising the
shame, and has sat down at the right hand of the throne of God.
Hebrews 12:2 (NIV)

Growing in faith is a process. We all have different measures of faith that
God has given us (Romans 12:3). It is not a competition as to who has
greater faith. Comparing our measure of faith with each other can leave
us either feeling prideful or like we don't measure up. We miss the big
picture if we do that. We all have different life experiences and each of our
relationships with Jesus looks different. We grow with Him in faith as we
take leaps towards the directions He shows us, and as we read the Bible
and apply what we learn (faith comes by hearing and hearing by the Word
of God - Romans 10:17). Our faith will continue to grow as we walk with
Jesus. He is the Author and Finisher of our faith. Keep in your lane and ask
Him to help you grow stronger on your faith journey with Him. Faith and
deeds go together. Don't be afraid to step out with Him, He will catch you.

Declaration: I don't compare my faith walk with others; I remain in my
lane and continue to grow in faith each day.

46

HE KNOWS YOU TO YOUR CORE

"Before I formed you in the womb I knew you, before you were
born I set you apart; I appointed you as a prophet to the nations."
Jeremiah 1:5 (NIV)

God knows who you are. Even before you took your first breath, He
already had a purpose and destiny for your life. God said to the prophet
Jeremiah that He set him apart and appointed him as a prophet before
he was even born! How amazing is that! We serve an awesome God! God
knows our past, our present and our future. No matter at what stage of life
you are in, know that the King of Kings and Lord of Lords knows 'you'. My
question to you though is, do you know God? I am not talking about having
knowledge of Him, I am talking about 'knowing' Him personally as the
love of your life? Do you take time to get to know Him and His nature? Do
you talk with Him as a friend and invite Him into every area of your life?
He is so worth getting to know! If you have not made it a priority to get to
know God on a personal level for yourself, then I would like to encourage
you to do so. You won't regret it!

Declaration: God knows me and has set me apart for Him.

47

RUN TOWARDS HIM WHEN YOU FALTER

But the Lord God called to the man, "Where are you?"
Genesis 3:9(NIV)

We were created to have a deep meaningful relationship with God. Even from the beginning, when God created Adam, God wanted to be a part of man's life. We read in Genesis that after the "fall", Adam and Eve hid from God. God, in His infinite love, knowing that Adam and Eve sinned against Him, still walked in the garden of Eden, calling out to Adam, asking him where he was. Adam admitted to God that he was hiding from Him because he was afraid. Are you hiding from God? Do you feel like you have to hide and run away from Him because you have sinned against Him? Are you afraid that He will be mad at you and push you away? God is not like man. He does not think as we do. His love for you is unconditional. He created you for Himself. His grace is abundant. Don't run from Him when you have sinned. Run towards Him. Ask Him to forgive you in Jesus name, and continue in your relationship with Him. There is no need to hide. God knows it all already.

Declaration: I don't run from God; He loves me.

48

GOD IS NOT A GENIE

God is Spirit, and those who worship Him
must worship in spirit and truth.
John 4:24 (NKJV)

God created us not only with a physical body but also with a spirit. It is our spirit that connects with God's Spirit on a deeper intimate level, establishing our relationship with Him. Our spirit forms part of our identity in Christ. But what does it mean to worship God in spirit and truth? The definition of "spirit" in the dictionary describes "spirit" as the typical quality, mood, attitude, and intention with which someone undertakes a task or regards something. So, when we worship, it is prudent for us to do a quick self-check regarding our attitude, intentions and our mood in which we worship God. Are we worshipping Him to "get" something from Him, or are we worshipping out of genuineness of love and adoration for Him? A good example of worshipping in the flesh vs worshipping in the spirit can be found in Luke 18:10-14. Is your heart truthful and genuine during worship? God desires for us to be authentic towards Him at all times.

Declaration: I worship God with the right attitude, intention and motive.

49

YOU ARE A KING AND A PRIEST

And hath made us kings and priests unto God and His Father;
to Him be glory and dominion for ever and ever. Amen.
Revelation 1:6 (KJV)

When you have given your life to Christ and made Jesus Lord and Saviour of your life, you not only receive the adoption of sonship, but you are also grafted in as king and priest in God's Kingdom. The Lord has given us the authority to rule over the earth and subdue it. Priests reflect service. Serving God's children faithfully with the gifts God gave us and also praying and interceding for others and standing in the "gap" to pray for mercy and repentance for others, our cities and nations. Kings reflect authority. As kings, we have the authority to decree God's purposes on the earth. As the Bible says, whatever we bind on earth will be bound in heaven and whatever we lose on earth is loosed in heaven. We do not make decrees out of our flesh or own desires, but rather we wait on God, and speak only that which He gives us to speak. Both priest and king work in partnership with God.

Declaration: I pray, serve and decree in accordance with God's Word.

50

GOD LOOKS AT THE HEART

Blessed are the pure in heart for they shall see God.
Matthew 5:8 (KJV)

What does purity of the heart mean? It is a yearning to do the right thing, to be quick and swift to repent when you recognize sin you committed. A stewardship of integrity and honesty. A willingness and diligence to pursue God and do things His way. To not harbour bitterness, unforgiveness or resentment in our hearts. To love our neighbour as ourselves. To keep our thoughts and actions pure. To keep our hands clean from gossip, betrayal, sin, lusts, pride, greed and worldly things. Jesus' sacrifice on the cross is there to cover our shortcomings when we don't do it perfectly, but we should have hearts that don't want to grieve His Holy Spirit. Hearts that would be sensitive to what would please God and what wouldn't please Him. Sensitivity to His heart is gained through intentional seeking. Spending time in prayer, waiting on Him and at His doors to listen to what He might say, and worshipping and spending time in the Bible. God is looking for pure hearts. Cultivate a pure heart out of love for Him.

Declaration: I aim to keep my heart pure before God.

51

A GOOD THING OR A GOD THING

Moses' father-in-law replied, "What you are doing is not good.
You and these people who come to you will only wear yourselves
out. The work is too heavy for you; you cannot handle it alone.
Exodus 18:17-18 (NIV)

Part of our identity in Christ is knowing and understanding how God is operating through us and how God wants to operate through us to reach others for Him. If we are not clear about what God is asking us to do, we can often "take on" more than what He asks or requires of us and the end result leads to overwhelm and burnout. It is hard, especially for leaders in the body of Christ to say "no" to "a good thing". People often expect us to do the "good things". However, not all "good things" are "God things". For example, it is a good thing to serve and help out. However, if God asked you to do something different, and you decide to do what God asked, and then you also serve and help where He didn't call, then you take on too much than what God intended for you. You will become unbalanced and quickly wear yourself out. God never intends for one person to carry all the burdens. It is okay to say no to "good things" when God has not called you to it. Don't allow the enemy or people to put guilt, shame, or condemnation on you. Know that you are free in Christ and are free to follow Him regardless of whether it pleases people or not.

Declaration: I work within the boundaries that God sets for me.

52

YOU ARE GRANTED AUTHORITY THROUGH HIM

"I tell you the truth, whatever you bind on earth
will be bound in heaven, and whatever you
loose on earth will be loosed in heaven."
Matthew 18:18 (NIV)

D o you know that when you accepted Jesus as Lord and Saviour of your
life, that you also received power and authority in Him? Not power and
authority to do as you please, but power and authority to rule and reign
on this earth as predetermined by Daddy-God. Jesus is the Name above
every Name. He has given us authority in His Name to bind the works
of Satan on this earth and to lose heaven here on earth. This is the task of
every believer and not just a few selected ones. Sometimes we become complacent and don't exercise our authority in Christ, and the result is greater
chaos and darkness roaming freely. You can make a difference by binding
the works of Satan and releasing heaven. For example, if there is a high rate
of crime in your area, bind and break in the name of Jesus the sprits and
demonic forces at work in your area, and then declare a loosening of the
peace of Christ in your area. See God work!

Declaration: I partner with Jesus to bind and loose in accordance with His
will.

www.ingramcontent.com/pod-product-compliance
Lightning Source LLC
LaVergne TN
LVHW051159080426

835508LV00021B/2706